To my amazing wife Rachel, and my parents for being my inspiration, writing these books would not have been possible without their support and love

Thank you

Carl

I0481609

## Foreword

I am a certified Project Management instructor with over 15 years' experience in Project and Program Management with various institutions from finance to aviation. I have experience of projects from small to multimillion pound projects

Throughout this journey I have attended multiple training courses for certification, and read numerous online articles and books, but the truth is that in most cases I have only ever understood part of the content, the book or the online material as the language was so obscure or the subject made overly complex, I wrote a book recently as a guide to Prince2 2017 and whilst writing it discussed the idea of a simpler guide to managing projects that can be understood quickly and the knowledge applied

I hope you find it useful and enjoyable, I tried to put my real-world experiences into it to support you

Thank you and good luck

Carl

# Project Management Made Simple

OK, so before we start, I have a confession! As my gorgeous wife will tell you, I have literally the smallest of attention spans and lose focus very easily, so this book is intended and purposely intended to be concise and to the point, there is very little fluff.

This book has been written in a compact format to ensure it focuses on what is the most important thing, making managing projects as simple and effective as possible and removing the jargon so that anyone can become a proficient and competent project manager

# The Basics!

So, before we start, let's set the scene and go through some of the basics,

## What is a project?

The various methodologies or guides have their own definition, and PMI says

"A project is a temporary endeavour to create a unique product or service"

whilst the Prince2 definition is

"A project is a temporary organisation that is created for the purpose of delivering one or more business products to an agreed business case"

The key in both is

- Temporary – projects have a defined start and an end
- Temporary organisation – the project team exists for the duration of the project and once it is completed is disbanded and possibly assigned to another project
- Unique – Each project is different, normal business operations are not project's, the creation of a product, house, car etc that would not be created if your project never existed is the project, it has a defined beginning and a defined end, and it creates one of a kind product
- Business Case – Each project should have an agreed business case and should deliver against that business case, it defines why you need the project and what the benefit that will be achieved because of the project

## What is Project Management?

In its most simple form, project management is the use of knowledge and methods to ensure the projects objectives are met or achieved, which translates to it is a process that when followed gives a greater chance of a successful project

## What does a Project Manager do?

The project manager is the often the only person assigned to the project full time, and represents the Executive or Sponsor, they are expected to:

- Lead the project Team
- Guide them on a daily basis
- Monitor and control the project against the approved plan and business case
- Manage and where possible resolve issues, risks, change requests as they arise, and when needed escalate them for guidance, advice or approvals
- Coordinate the project activities and team members
- Communicate to project stakeholders – both internal and external to the project

**What are the skills needed to be a project manager?**
I always joke about this when I teach and explain that some of the most effective tools a project manager needs, are the ability to communicate and garner trust of those around and the best example of this is a second-hand car salesman, within 15 minutes of meeting him, you have bought a car, agreed to a warranty plan you never knew you needed and your friends on Facebook! How is this possible, because he is an effective communicator and knows how to develop trust quickly?

The project manager should possess or be capable of:

- Planning and coordination
- Estimating
- Financial management, budgeting
- The ability to problem solve
- The ability to delegate
- Effective communication skills

There are arguments about the final one, which is domain knowledge or specialist knowledge, my personal opinion that a good project manager should be able to effectively manage any project unless it is a very technical or specialist project. However, the argument that having domain or specialist knowledge allows the project manager to be more effective quickly, speak the right language and quickly build trust with the stakeholders

**Project Objectives**

The project is delivered against a set of objectives, Prince2 calls these the Project Objectives or Variables, and these are:

1. *Time* – How long will it take to deliver and when will we realise the benefits
2. *Cost* – How much will it cost to deliver and how much will it cost to maintain
3. *Quality* – How will ensure the product delivered is fit for purpose
4. *Scope* – what are you delivering and more importantly, what aren't you delivering
5. *Risk* – How much risk is acceptable to deliver the project and achieve the benefits
6. *Benefits* – why are we doing this project, what will we gain

**How is the project broken down?**

A project is broken into what are known as stages or phases, this allows the Project Board to maintain effective control and ask the right questions when transitioning from one stage or phase to another

These questions are

- Is the project still viable, achievable and desirable?
- Does the project remain justified, is it still in line with the approved Business Case?
- Is the project where is should be against the approved plan

The normal stages of a project are:

1. Start-Up – often classed as pre-project as there is no approved Business Case
2. Initiation – can be combined with Start-Up in some organisations
3. Delivery, which can also be known as execution and includes the monitoring and control
4. Closing

The stages or the project are sequential, and the stages above should only be delivered in the sequence above, it is also important to understand that there can only be one of each stage running at any point in the project.

The Start-Up stage can also be broken into phases in a complicated project for example, if you have to confirm project requirements, run an RFP to select a vendor or 3$^{rd}$ party, finalise the Business Case (updated based upon the vendor selection and the updated or revised costs) and obtain approvals, each of these could be a separate stage within the Start-Up phase, however until you request permission to transition to delivery, the project remains in Start-Up

In projects that are iterative, stages 2, 3 and 4 could be completed multiple times and this process could allow for benefits to be achieved in a staggered fashion, thus providing a quicker return of investment (ROI)

The project process used within this book is based upon the classic waterfall method, which is a sequentially planned and delivered project, it is also the most popular method with organisations

## Starting the Project

So, what is the purpose of a controlled start to a project, why waste the time when you're then going to start planning it anyway?

The answer is simple, the purpose is to obtain approval for the project and officially confirm that your organisation agrees that the project is worthwhile and that it is aligned to the organisations strategic objectives

The second part of the answer is to stop projects that are not achievable or aligned to those objectives from starting, this ensures that the resources are delivering the right projects

The Start-Up stage aims to answer 4 main questions, these being:

1   **What?**
      a.   What are the deliverables,
      b.   What are the objectives

This question is focused upon the deliverables of the project and aims to clarify the Project Scope. For the project to succeed it must deliver a product that is fit for purpose and enables the objectives to be met, anything that is not included in the scope that is delivered is considered as either a change or scope creep

Changes to the scope or deliverables should be approved through a structured process to ensure that only those changes that enable the products to be delivered and deliver benefits should be approved

Scope Creep should be avoided at all costs, Scope Creep is a classic reason for project failure as it uses resources (physical manpower, time, money etc)

## 2 Why?
    a.   Why should we do this project?

The reasons for the project should be clearly understood, is the project needed to resolve an issue, or meet a need that has been identified, or is it a regulatory project that must be delivered to ensure the organisation remains active or process within the organisation can continue?

It is key that the project manager always ensures the reason for the project is understood by all stakeholders involved in the project and that it remains at the forefront.

## 3 When?
    a.   When will we deliver the products?
    b.   When will the benefits be realised?

This simple question allows the project manager to understand the time required to both deliver the project and for the products delivered to enable the realisation of the identified benefits

## 4 Who?
    a.   Who is impacted by this project?

b. Who is involved with this project?
c. Who is responsible for this project and the benefits?

These people are called stakeholders, the definition of a stakeholder is "any person who is affected or perceives themselves to be affected by the projects outcome"

In projects you can have both positive stakeholders who openly support your project and the products being delivered and you can have negative stakeholders who are not supportive or perceive that your project will have a negative impact upon them in some way

It is key to the success of your project to identify both sets of stakeholders and understand their individual needs

By answering the What, Why, When and Who, the project manager can define what the project is and its justification. This should then be documented within the Business Case with the options of:
- Do Nothing – remain as you are – also known as the status quo
- Do Minimum – where the products delivered meet the minimum viable proposition
- Do Something – which is a middle ground between doing nothing and doing the minimum

The Business Case should also include the schedule and the estimated costs for the delivery of the project, the schedule and the costs should be derived from workshops where the project manager is supported by Subject Matter Experts to create both the project plan or schedule and also understand what resources are needed to deliver the project. Only with this information can viable estimate be created. The project manager should never create the schedule or estimate in isolation, this will lead to an unclear plan and possibly unachievable timelines

The contents of the Case should ideally be:
1. Executive Summary
   a. High level overview of the project incorporating the Time, Cost, Quality, Scope, Benefits and Risks

2. Reasons
    a. The justification for the project


3. Business options
    a. Do nothing
    b. Do the minimum
    c. Do something
4. Expected benefits
    a. Benefits should be tangible and measurable (where possible should be measurable in a Yes or No)
5. Expected dis-benefits
    a. Any negative impacts that may arise from the implementation of the projects products
6. Timescales
7. Costs
8. Investment appraisal
9. Major Risks

The Business Case is possibly the most important document once approved, and is the document that the Project Manager will review on a regular basis when assessing the impact of change requests, risks or issues as any of these could mean the project is no longer justifiable and therefore no longer value for money

During the Start-Up Phase the project manager will undertake the following tasks or activities,

- Identify the answers to the What, Why, When and who, possibly from the Project Executive or Sponsor and documents these
- Creates a draft Business Case containing the information above
- Create the Project Organisation or Project Structure, which at this stage will simply identify the roles needed within the project and possibly only contain the Project Executive and project manager as identified resources assigned to the project
- Form the Project Steering Committee or Board, this would normally comprise of the

- o The Project Executive or Sponsor – who is ultimately responsible for the project's success
- o The Senior User – who represents the needs of those who will use the products delivered by the project
- o The Senior Supplier – who represents those specialists who create or build the projects products
- Update the Business Case and submit for approval by the Project Steering Committee or Board
- Create a Project Charter
  - o The Project Charter provides a high-level overview of the project, think of it a 1 pager on the entire project and it could include:
    - Project ID (name, Description)
    - Project Organisation
    - What, Why, When and Who
    - Budget

Once the Business Case and Project Charter are approved, the project manager can officially commence the project (In a Prince2 project, until the Business Case is approved it is not an official project!) and can utilise the approved budget

Once the documents are approved, they are then baselined and use as a measure to ascertain the project overall success. In the event that there are changes to the project or its products, the Business Case and Project Charter should be updated to ensure they always reflect the most up to date and accurate information regarding the projects schedule, finances, products and benefits

The project manager will now create a stage plan for the next project stage, it is always recommended to have a high-level plan for the Project Board and a detailed stage plan for the project manager to use for the day-2-day management of the projects and monitoring\tracking its progress.

This Stage Plan should be created close to the end of the current stage and should form part of the control process of transitioning from one stage to another

This transition process is called a Stage Gate, where the organisation, typically the Corporate Project Management Office and a member of the Project Board will conduct a review of the project and confirm it is being delivered in line with any organisational standards, remains in-line with the approved Business Case, that the next stage is planned and clearly understood, it also serves as a control function for the Project Board to assert control and understand the project and its progress to date

Once approved to proceed to the next stage, the project manager will schedule a Project Kick-Off meeting and typically include the Project Board, any major stakeholders and the project delivery team. The purpose of the meeting is to ensure that all stakeholders and fully aware of the project, its justification, schedule and objectives

This meeting officially confirms the project has started and is approved

## Initiation

The project has now been approved along with the approved Business Case and Project Charter, the next stage is aimed at answering the question

**How?**

- How will we deliver the project?
- How will we achieve the projects objectives?

The project manager will use the high-level project plan that was created to support the creation of the Business Case and the Project Charter to start to answer the questions

- What are we delivering? and How will it resolve the problem(s) identified? and meet the needs of the user community? Within the allotted objectives of Time, Cost, Quality

The project manager will undertake a number of tasks  or activities as with the Starting-Up stage to complete the Initiation stage

The project manager will identify the specific project deliverables, these are the specialist products that will be delivered by your project, this is best completed using the process of workshops again with Subject Matter Experts.  The starting point is the end product that will be delivered, and this is then broken down into as many components as possible, for example if you are building a house, the house is the end product and the sub products would look like this

1. Completed House
    1.1. Foundation
    1.2. Windows
    1.3. Electrical Supply
    1.4. Plumbing
    1.5. Kitchen
    1.6. Bathrooms
    1.7. Garage

Each of the subtasks would then have their own individual sub tasks and at this level they are call Work Packages or Statements of Work depending upon your organisation

The process of breaking products down like this is called a Product Breakdown Structure and would look something like the diagram below

Once the project manager understands the main product to be delivered and the sub products that are needed to complete this, the understanding each of those items and the dependencies and creation\development cycle can then determine the types of resources and the processes needed for each of those sub products

For example, the resources needed to create and install the foundations of a house are very different from those who will create and install the windows

This information will form the basis for the delivery team, the specialists that are needed to deliver the actual project

Once the project manager understands the products, the next question to ask is how long will it take to deliver or create them?

For each of the activities identified, the next step is again undertaken with the Subject Matter Experts to understand how long each will take to deliver. These estimates are never 100% accurate and should always be listed with any assumptions associated with the delivery and of course, the project manager will understand that these assumptions could also be translated into risks that could affect the actually delivery and impact any of the objects (Time, Cost, Scope, Quality, Risks and Benefits)

It may also be possible to use data from previous projects, which would be more accurate than method above, but this depends upon the availability of the data, which is aligned to the maturity of the organisation

There is also the method of using the Best Case, Most Likely Case and Worst Case, this is called a PERT analysis which stands for Project Evaluation and Review Technique. This was developed by the US Navy in the 1950's in conjunction with the Critical Path Method (CPM) as part of the Polaris nuclear submarine project and has been widely adopted

The project manager now understands more about the products and the time needed to deliver them along with any assumptions that could affect the delivery and also affect the project objectives, this can now be developed into the project schedule

Once the project schedule is understood and has been documented, most likely in MS Project the next task is to understand the Critical Path, in its most simplistic definition, the Critical Path is the longest sequence of activities in a project schedule that must be completed on time to enable the project to be completed on time, this demonstrates the minimum time needed to deliver the project and also indicates the activities with the highest risk associated or dependencies attached to them

The schedule when entered into MS Project will provide the project manager with the classic understanding of a project plan, the Gannt Chart which is effectively a bar chart depicting the project schedule, as illustrated below

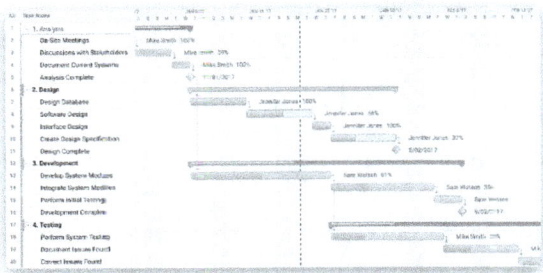

Ok, so we now have a clear understanding of what we are delivering, how we deliver it, how long it will take and what resources are needed, the next question and often the one that is most objected is how much will it costs?

The project manager again with the Subject Matter Experts will create a cost estimate for each of the activities, this will form the estimated project budget and should align to the approved Business Case created in the Start-Up Phase, however in most organisation where the project process includes a Start-Up and Initiation Stage, the Business Case created in Start-Up is based upon a high level estimates (in some organisations this can be as high as plus or minus 50% on the estimates submitted) and the Business Case is then revised and resubmitted as part of the Project Initiation Documentation as the Final Business Case, these are often termed Outline Business Case and Detailed Business Case or BC1 and BC2

The project manager will also try and answer more questions that are aligned to the project objectives as the plan answers the Time, Cost and Scope predominantly, leaving Quality, Risk and Benefits

So, let's look at Quality, the project manager needs to understand the Customers Quality Expectations, what does good look like, how will the product be used, and this information will allow the product delivered by the project to be fit for purpose and meet those expectations

Understanding those quality expectations also allows the project manager to understand how the products will be measured, what is needed to measure them and most importantly who will measure them to confirm they meet the expectations and are fit for purpose

So now we have Risks and Benefits remaining, so let's look at risks

what is a risk? The Prince2 definition is

"An uncertain event or set of events that, should it occur will have an effect on the achievement of benefits"

So, in essence a risk is something that has not yet happened, but if it does will have an impact on the projects objectives. The project manager should manage risk using a document called a Risk Register, which is a central repository for all information relating to risks and their ongoing management, the risk register should contain (ideally)

- Unique risk ID
- Risk author (Who raised the risk)
- Date raised
- Risk category (for example: People, Process, Technology, Finance, Schedule etc.)
- Probability (of the risk occurring)
- Impact (of the risk upon the project objectives at risk)
- Proximity (stage, project, activity)
- Rask rating (which is a combination of the probability and impact)
- Risk response (the action to be taken to reduce either the probability, impact or both)
- Risk owner (the person responsible for the monitoring the risk and taking out the risk management action if it occurs)
- Risk status (open\closed)
- Remarks

Understanding the risk in relation to its probability and impact is simplified using a probability and impact matrix as illustrated below

The left hand of the graph is based upon the probability of the risk occurring, what are the chances it will actually happen, and the bottom is based upon the impact if it does occur

When combined these provide the project manager with a risk rating and those in the top right quadrant will obviously need more rigorous management actions and possibly escalation to the project board or steering group

Risk management is the responsibility of the project manager and should be constantly undertaken throughout the project, it is the responsibility of the project manager to maximize the chances of positive risks and reduce or eliminate the negative risks. It is important to constantly monitor the risks and assess new risks as they arise throughout the whole life of the project

This now leaves us with the Benefits, which is most organisations will be the area that is often the most visible when writing a Business Case and justification for a project

So, what are the benefits? In the most simplistic term it is the change derived from the projects products, and in Prince2 for example it says it is an outcome that is advantageous to an individual or group

That could be reduction in costs, increased revenue, better services, improved processes or a mix of any of the above.

These benefits are known as tangible benefits which means they can be defined, baselined and measured against to demonstrate an improvement

A non-tangible benefit is not so easy to measure as they are subjective or based upon a perception, for example HR may say a project could provide the benefit of improved employee morale, which is subjective and individual. If I have had a bad night's sleep and I am in a bad mood, when I get the survey looking at my morale, my responses will be possibly negative but nothing to do with the project

When your defining the benefits, it is key to understand:
- The benefit being delivered – process improvement, manpower reduction etc.
- The baseline – that the benefit will be measured against and when that will be documented
- How it will be measured
- Are any specialist tools or date needed to measure the benefits?
- Who will measure the benefit?
- When will it be measured
- Who needs this information and when?
- What format the Benefits reports will be in?

The project manager will obtain the majority of this information from the Project Executive\Sponsor and Senior User who represents the end users of the specialist products or the change being delivered

This will all then be documented into the Benefits Management Plan and included in the Business Case, which again should be updated with all of the latest information now that you know a lot more about the project and as previously explained this will probably be in what's called the Detailed Business Case or BC2

You have now identified, the Products, dependencies and schedule to deliver or create them, the cost estimates and updated the Business Case and the Benefits Management Plan.

Now let's look at the stakeholders as you know more about the project and its key stakeholders

Remember the definition of a stakeholder is any persons who is affected or perceives themselves to be affected by the projects outcome, as you have engaged with Subject Matter Experts and the Project Board\Steering Group, you have identified people with both positive and negative views of the project. So now the project manager will underetake a stakeholder analysis

- For each stakeholder identified during the Start-Up and Initiating Phase, determine their level of power through their authority or influence on the project, and then determine their actual interest in the project. This is best done using a Power Vs Interest Grid as illustrated below:

- The Power Vs Interest grid is a simple tool that helps project managers categorize stakeholders and understand their influence on the project

Once the project manager understands the stakeholders and where they sit within the grid, the next step is determining the approach to communicate with the various stakeholder groups, it is key to ensure that stakeholders who have high power and interest within the project are documented as main stakeholders and the communication with them should be given a priority and they should be engaged closely

The list of stakeholders should be documented in the Project Communication Plan

This is effectively all of the planning to deliver the project undertaken and you are at or near the end of the Initiation stage of the project, which should trigger a control point or sage gate for the Project Board or Steering Group to make a decision and reaffirm the project continues to be justified and represents value for money

This will be done using the Project Initiation Document (PID), which is often a presentation that summaries the project in a similar fashion to the Project Charter but contains more detail, it acts as the foundation for the project and will again list the

- Why are we undertaking this project?
- What are we delivering?
- Who is responsible?
- When will we deliver it? and when will we see the benefits?

A good PID should contain all of the above and also include

- The Project Organisation
- Major Risks
- Assumptions or Constraints
- Reporting Process

And most importantly an Executive Summary giving an overview of all of the above in a simple and concise manner

As with the Starting-Up stage, the project manager will create a stage plan for the next stage, which is often known as the delivery stage, In Prince2 this is known as the Next Stage Plan or Delivery Stage Plan and is a Plan that allows the project manager to manage the stage on a day-2-day basis and will be submitted with the PID to the Project Board for approval to proceed to the next stage and close the Initiation Stage

So, the activities the project manager has undertaken in this stage are:

1. Create the Project Plan
2. Documented the Product Breakdown Structure
3. Refined the Business Case
4. Create the Risk Register

5. Created the Benefits Management Plan
6. Created the Communication Management Plan
7. Create the Project Initiation Document
8. Obtained approval to proceed to the delivery stage

## Delivery Stage

After completing the Start-Up and Initiation Stage, its now finally time to actually deliver the projects products and do what is in effect the task of the project manager.

At this point the project manager should have a very clear understanding of the project, its outputs and the process to deliver them.

The project manager will use the Product Breakdown Structure to create the Product Descriptions for each of the products and its associated sub products, this process supports the creation of the Work Packages for the actual product creation\delivery

The Product Description should contain (as a minimum)

- Unique product identifier
- Product title
- Purpose
- Composition – what products make up this product
- Derivation – where is the information derived or sourced from to create this product description
- Development skills – physical resources or tools needed
- Quality
    - Quality criteria – what does good look like
    - Quality tolerances – are there any tolerances that relate to the product
    - Quality method – how will it be measured
    - Quality skills – what skills are needed to measure the product
    - Quality responsibilities – who is approved to review and accept the product

The project manager will create the product descriptions again with support from Subject Matter Experts to ensure they are as accurate as possible, remembering this information will be used to create the

Work Packages that will be used by the delivery teams (the specialists) who will create\develop\build the project products

The project manager will then review the current requirements, the process of gathering the requirements is undertaken using various tools, for example: Workshops, 1-2-1 meetings, process reviews and is often undertaken by team members or project members acting a Business Analysts, who will gather the detailed business requirements, success criteria and quality criteria. This set of requirements enables the project manager to determine the continued viability of the project and that it can continue to meet the customers' expectations

The requirements can be documented in a number of ways, the simplest of which is a statement of requirements, which can be then linked to requirements traceability matrix. This is a simple table that links the business requirements with the design, test cases, test results. This matrix allows the project manager to map the user requirements to the associated test case and thus ensuring that no functionality is missed – see illustration below

Most projects are a customer supplier-based projects, and the supplier will assign a project manager to the project to manage the delivery the specialist products, for simplicity we will call them the team manager (which is a Prince2 term) rather than saying the project manager will assign the work package to the project manager, which will become confusing for you and even more confusing for me writing it

In some projects this may mean that the actual delivery of the projects products must be outsourced and therefore a procurement process must be followed to select this 3rd party or vendor

This would normally be identified during the Initiation Stage and the project manager would identify the deliverables, activities and processes required to complete this process. This will normally take the form of a Request for Quotation (RFQ) or Request for Proposal (RFP), these are based upon the known and agreed requirements and the vendors will then respond

These responses will be evaluated, again as with all things the project manager should be supported by Subject Matter Experts and in this case, ideally include procurement and finance (and possibly legal) to evaluate any contractual and financial details contained within the responses. The responses are evaluated and reviewed to ascertain which meets the business requirements and project objectives in relation to Time and Cost best. The work will then be awarded to the selected vendor or vendors and a contractual obligation put in place, it should be noted that the procurement process will vary between organisations and the project manager should review the internal processes to ensure the project remains within the organisations governance processes and procedures. This is especially important when awarding contracts with financial value associated

There are different types of contract, but the most common are:
- Fixed Price –
    - Best suited to be used when the scope of work is clearly understood and the there is little chance of changes
    - Upon contract signature, the vendor is liable for the delivery of the products according to the agreed contract for a fixed fee
    - In this type of contract, the vendor bears the majority of the risks as there is often a penalty clause for not meeting the requirements or objective of Time

- Cost Reimbursement
  - The most common type of contract, where the vendor is reimbursed for the work completed plus an additional fee for their services or resources
  - This can be used if the scope is not so well defined and can be completed in stages to allow that definition to be clarified
  - Can be problematic for the project manager when auditing finances for work completed by the vendor
  - Risks are assumed by the project in this type of contract as the project is liable for the costs
    - The only caveat is once the requirements and statement are agreed – the vendor will be measured against those

- Time and Materials
  - This is often used when a contract is in place with a vendor and you are only using them for periods of time or specific resources
  - The project manager must track this type of contract more diligently to track actuals versus estimates in relation to time\effort and costs associated

The vendor is now in place and working on the project, the project manager will create the draft Work Package with the team leader, using a process of review and negotiation the team manager will accept the work package and agree to deliver it.

The work package is a group of related tasks within the project that in themselves look like projects, they can often be thought of as sub-projects within a larger project. Work packages are the smallest unit of work that the project can be broken down into and are derived from the Product Breakdown Structure and the Product Descriptions

The work package should contain the following information
- Work Package ID (ideally linked to the Product Description)

- Description
- Team Manager Details
- Techniques\Processes\Procedures
- Development Interfaces
- Operations\Maintenance Interfaces
- Configuration Management Requirements
- Tolerances
- Constraints
- Quality (derived directly from the Product Description)
  - Quality criteria – what does good look like
  - Quality tolerances – are there any tolerances that relate to the product
  - Quality method – how will it be measured
  - Quality skills – what skills are needed to measure the product
  - Quality responsibilities – who is approved to review and accept the product
- Reporting requirements
- Problem handling\escalation
- Approval requirements

As determined above, the team manager will accept the work package, and the project manager will grant approval to deliver it. At this point the team manager will as documented in the Work Package update the project manager as to the status of the development or creation of the product aligned to the Work Package. This is in the form of the Checkpoint Report.

The team manager will then perform the tasks or work required to produce the required products, this is often completed by specialists (builders, electricians, IT Developers etc.)

The project manager will monitor and track the work to ensure the project remains with the tolerances agreed and the project objectives (Time, Cost, Scope, Quality, Risk, Benefits) and as documented within the Work Package. This is known as Monitoring and Control

Once the team manager has completed the creation of the products listed within the Work Package, they will need to be tested.

The project will perform testing, and this is normally undertaken by representatives of the Senior User, as the recipients or users of the end product. The testing will ensure that the products meet the stakeholder's quality expectations and that it is fit for purpose. In the event a product fails a test or fails to meet defined criteria, then the team manager will need to perform fixes and submit the product for re-testing until it meets the criteria and is deemed fit for purpose

In the event the products being delivered are required to integrate with a 3rd party or existing systems or services, then integration testing will need to be conducted to again ensure that the products are fit for purpose and meet the agreed or defined criteria and ensure they work seamlessly with the existing components or services.

Upon confirmation that all of the testing has been completed the project manager will normally schedule the final acceptance testing, which is often known as User Acceptance testing or Operational Readiness Testing, this is conducted by larger groups of stakeholders to ensure that the product is fit for purpose and the documented requirements are met.

In the event a product fails to meet those requirements, the project manager can
- Obtain user feedback to understand what is incorrect, why and the impact
- Identifies and documents the area for improvement
- Determines any corrections required
- Assesses the possible impact on the project schedule and costs
- Raise a defect against the failure and
- Assign the defect to the team manager for resolution

Once the defect has been resolved, the project manager will arrange for re-testing to be undertaken until the product meets the full set of requirements and quality criteria

It is worth noting that in most projects where User Acceptance Testing is required, it is more often the case that 2 or 3 sessions will be conducted before the product is agreed to be fit for purpose

## Monitoring and Control

Monitoring and control is not a stage in itself but is a group of activities that are undertaken to ensure the project remains on track and is progressing as per the project and stage plan. The activities span the project from Start-Up, Initiation and the Delivery Stages.

The earlier any deviation or issue is detected and understood, the easier it is to remedy this and put the project back on track. Anything can wrong on a project, let's remember projects introduce change and by that nature, they are open to change, in almost 20 years I have never had a project that did not have a change request raised.

The requirements traceability matrix can be used along with the Product Descriptions by the project manager assess the impact of changes as they provide a link between the products, the design and the test cases. This enables the project manager to fully understand the change and its impact.

Project managers need to also understand that things go wrong, especially in large, complex projects and the project manager should monitor the objectives (Time, Cost, Scope, Quality, Risk, Benefits) and constantly compare the projects progress against both the project plan and stage plan to ensure the project is proceeding as planned, when tracking the objectives, the project manager will monitor:

- Scope
  - By monitoring and controlling the project scope, the project manager is effectively safeguarding against scope creep – where additional unapproved requirements are added to the projects scope, that are beyond the originally agreed scope and deliverables
  - Over-Delivery or Gold Plating – by providing more than was requested or agreed in the requirement. The expenditure of additional resources in either time\effort\costs spent in delivering a gold-plated solution will be wasted if the solution delivered is not agreed and over specified. By ensuring the solution that is

delivered is fit for purpose, and only what is needed is delivered the project manager ensures that the team is focused upon only what matters and what will ensure the project is deemed a success and the products delivered are fit for purpose

- Time or schedule
  - o The project manager will monitor the projects overall progress against the baselined project plan and stage plan and ensuring it is where it should be at, think of it as asking – are we where we should be?
- Costs
  - o The project manager will monitor the project spend based upon the approved and available budget. The project manager will monitor this based upon
    - The approved Business Case
    - The approved contract and contractual milestones
  - o This will be reported upon as
    - Forecasted Spend – what was agreed as the project budget and the schedule of payments or spend
    - Actual – the actual payments made
    - Remaining – what is remaining of the budget
  - o If this monitoring highlights any concerns the project manage can:
    - Seek additional funds by submitting a change request or business case amendment depending upon the value or the organisational processes
    - Reduce the project scope, however this should be assessed in relation to the impact upon the projects overall justification and possible impact upon benefits and may also need the approval of the Project Board or Steering Group, is

exceptional circumstances it may need organisation approval

- Quality
    - o Ensuring that the projects products are fit for purpose and meets the customers quality expectations
- Risks
    - o External conditions change, and these may affect the project, these should be added to the risk register
        - For example, if your organisation is an Airline, the price of oil could negatively or positively impact your project, and this is an external condition that is a risk
    - o Existing risks should also be constantly reviewed and monitored to asses and understand if the proposed mitigation addresses the risks and reduces the probability or impact, if not then the mitigation should be reviewed and new one possibly required
- Contractual Obligation
    - o If the project has chosen to outsource the delivery of products that are required, the project manage should ensure that a review is undertaken against the contract and the work package and ensure that the 3rd party delivers the products according the contract and in line with the customers quality expectations
    - o If any deviation is identified, the project manager should seek to remediate this with the 3rd party, using clauses contained within the contract
- Communication
    - o The project manager should ensure that all identified stakeholders are on "the same page"" in relation to the project and its products. This ensures there are no surprises relating to the project
    - o It ensures the project manager manages the expectations of the stakeholders by controlling the

communications and the messages relating to the project
- Resources (People)
    - This the one area that should NEVER be neglected. the success of the project is dependent upon the project team and its ability to both work together and communicate, without this no project will ever succeed. The project manager should strive to constantly engage with the team and gauge the team's morale, confidence in the project and understanding of its goals

To support the process of Monitoring and Control, the project manager should:

Create and maintain an issue log, in most projects or organisations this is part of the Risk Register and known as the Risk, Actions\Assumptions, Issues, Dependencies log or register and allows the project manager to capture, assess, propose\implement a solution or resolution to the identified issue

The project manager should track
- **Scope**
    - Comparing detailed requirements against the baselines and the Product Breakdown Structure, this can aid the project manager in preventing scope creep and gold plating
    - If a change to a requirement is raised, the project manager should capture the information and assess the impact to the project, its resources, costs, schedule and against the Business Case and its justification. The project manager if required will the Project Board or Steering Group and make them aware of the impact analysis and if required seek approval for the issue
    - If the project manager detects scope creep, this should be assessed as to the impact upon the project and advises the person who requested the

change. If this is still required, then the project manager will seek approval to proceed with the requirement and accept its impact upon the project

- **Schedule**
  - The project manager will monitor the projects progress against the baseline plan ensuring it is progressing as planned. In the event it is not, then it will be assessed against the impact upon the overall project timeline
  - If the project timeline is affected or impacted and the project end date is potentially compromised the project manager will identify the issue and attempt to resolve it
  - If the issue cannot be resolved, the project manager can and should use the means available to ensure the project gets back on track, for example:
    - Fast tracking – performing multiple activities simultaneously
    - Resources – adding additional resources to the impacted area
    - Scope – reduction of project scope

- **Costs**
  - The project manager should track project expenses, comparing actuals versus forecasted and against the remaining costs to deliver the project ensuring the project finances are understood and any potential deviations are identified
  - Any deviations that could impact the project budget, this should be identified and escalated to the Project Board or Steering Group

- **Quality**
  - The project manager monitors the build\development process against the agreed requirements against the acceptance criteria to ensure the product quality and it remains fit for purpose
  - In the event any tests fail, the root cause needs to be identified

- The project manage can use the requirements traceability matrix to ensure that all deliverables are delivered against the user requirements
- The project manager should also collect feedback from stakeholders to assess areas for improvement and ways to enhance or speed up the delivery

- **Risks**
  - Using the Risk Register, the project manager should constantly review and assess the risks that are under management ensuring they have adequate mitigations to reduce the probability and\or impact
  - Negative risks can be – Avoided, Mitigated, accepted in the most basic risk responses
  - Positive risks if identified should be maximized by the project manager

- **Procurement**
  - The 3rd party vendor should be monitored against the agreed contract and or work package
  - The deliverables should be tested against the agreed quality criteria as documented within
    - Product Descriptions
    - Work Package

- **Communications**
  - It is imperative that the project manager creates an effective communication management plan to ensure there is a single message consistently portrayed
  - The project manage r should setup a common repository or folder that is accessible by all stakeholders
  - The project manager should communicate regularly to the project stakeholders ensuring a common understanding of what's coming next and that there are no surprises

- **People\Project Team**
  - This is often overlooked under the misguided concept that they are being paid so they should do

what is needed, which is the worst possible attitude a project manager should have

- The project manage should have frequent meetings and 1-to-1 meetings to understand team morale and obtain feedback, it is often advised to complete these meetings in an informal environment where team members will be more open to talk and express their true feelings
- Build and maintain trust, any items discussed that are confidential, remain confidential and should be recorded and indicated as their status
- When feedback is received from team members, the project manager should document this and act up it, feedback unless confidential the feedback should remain open and available to all members of the project

## Closing the Project

As explained, projects have a defined start and end. The project manager must officially close the project and the purpose of the closing phase is to close the project in a controlled manner and release the project resources

Project closure must be done, this is regardless of the success or failure of the project, if a project is prematurely closed then the products that have been completed should be assessed as to their viability and usefulness to the business or organization

The closing process ensures that the project products are officially accepted by the stakeholders (this is regardless of the closure method planned or premature)

Project resources are released in a controlled fashion, and any outstanding invoices are clarified and scheduled for payment

Organisational notification that the project has been closed and resources released

Lessons learned are documented and provided to organisation PMO

The project manager should
- Obtain all acceptance of the project deliverables
- Inform all resources managers of the projects closure and the release date of the resources
- Close any procurement processes
- Confirm that all invoices and project expenses can be finalised and processed
- Close finance accounts
- Update project documentation and complete the project review against the baselined documentation
- Collect feedback from project members and suggestions for improvements (to be included in the lessons learned)
- Schedule the Benefits Review aligned to the Benefits Management Plan
- Schedule Post Project Implementation Review (what went well, what went badly)
- Most importantly – Thank the project team for the support and work during the project

www.ingramcontent.com/pod-product-compliance
Lightning Source LLC
Chambersburg PA
CBHW070931220526
45468CB00005B/1736